HOW TO DRAW
ANIMALS
Learn to Draw with Grids for Kids

H.R. Wallace Publishing
hrwallacepublishing.com

Copyright © 2019 by H.R. Wallace. All rights reserved. No part of this book may be reproduced or transmitted in any form or by any means whatsoever without written permission from the publisher.

Every effort has been made to ensure that this book is complete and accurate. However, no responsibility is assumed for any human error, typographical mistakes, or any consequences resulting from the use of this book. The material in this book is provided "as is" without warranty of any kind.

Images used under license from Shutterstock.com

ISBN-10: 1-5091-0258-2
ISBN-13: 978-1-5091-0258-7

What's the Grid Method?

The grid method of drawing is great for beginners, because it breaks an image down into bite-sized pieces. By concentrating on copying an image one square at a time, artists can more easily create realistic line drawings, which means that young artists will be able to enjoy drawing over 25 cute animals with ease in no time at all.

As a matter of fact, many realism artists use the grid method to create their works of art, so it's a great technique for all aspiring artists to learn.

Drawing with the Grid Method

To use the grid method, start by looking at box A1 and then draw whatever you see in that square. Next, move on to box A2 and draw what you see there too.

Keep moving from box to box focusing only on drawing what you see in each little square. Continue moving through the rows until you finally reach box F7. Once you add in any details from that square, your drawing will be complete!

Practice Makes Perfect

Don't be discouraged if your drawing doesn't look quite right after your first, second, or even third attempt. The great thing about drawing is that the more you practice, the better you become, which means that with each attempt you will become more skilled as an artist. So, just keep practicing and, before you know it, you will be able to draw all sorts of animals.

Drawing Supplies

The number of tools available to artists may seem daunting, but the good news is that you only need a few basic items to complete these drawings.

Pencil

Pencils vary from very soft to hard and each is suited to a particular use. For the purposes of this book, however, a standard writing pencil, labeled #2/HB, will do nicely.

Eraser

An eraser is great for correcting mistakes. A vinyl eraser is recommended. This type of eraser is non-abrasive, which means that it won't damage your paper. It's also well-suited to erasing light marks and for precision erasing, so you should find that it works nicely.

Let's Start Drawing!

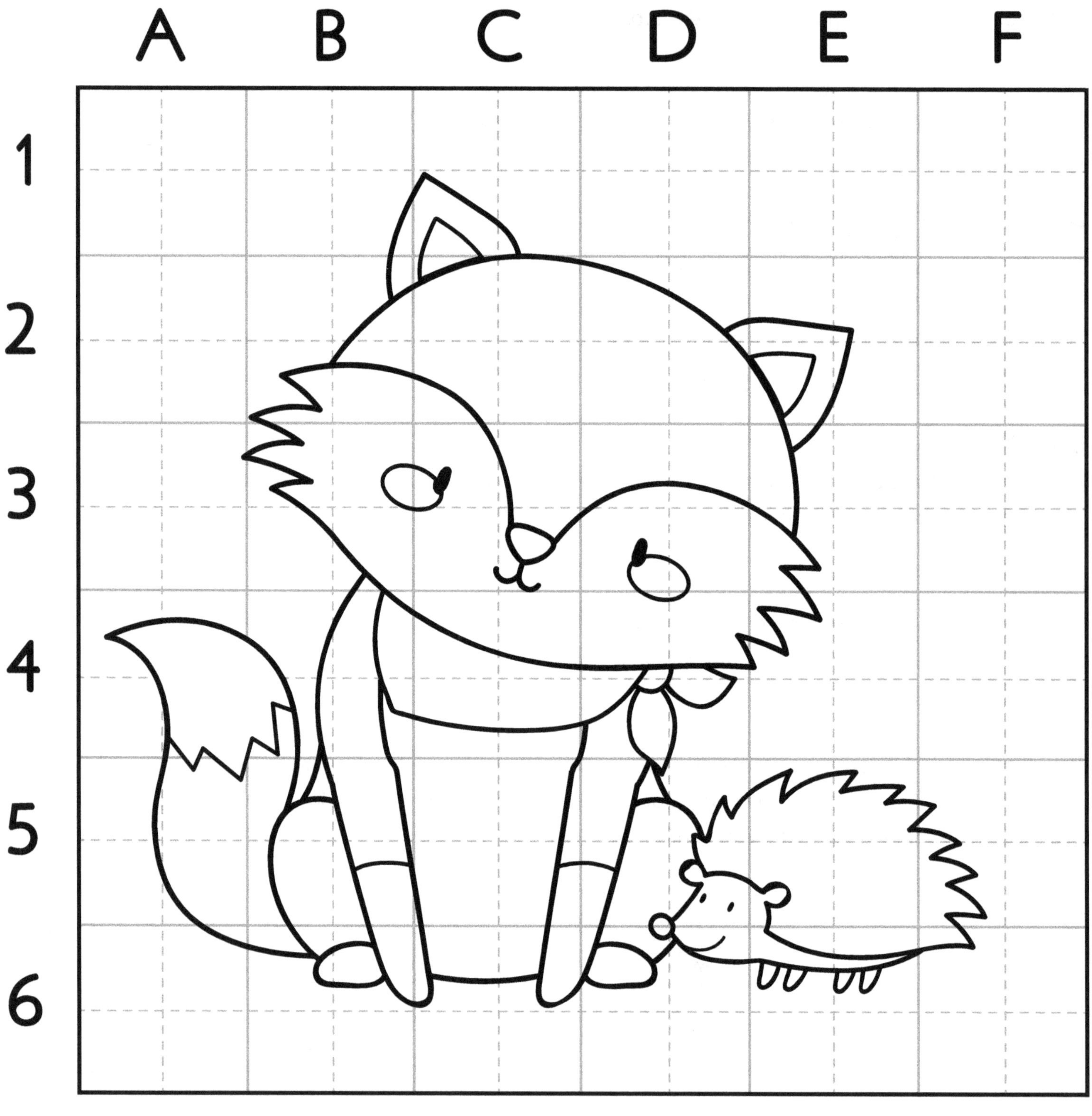

Draw the picture in the grid

	A	B	C	D	E	F
1						
2						
3						
4						
5						
6						

 Trace the fox & the hedgehog for more practice!

 Practice drawing the picture on your own!

Bunny

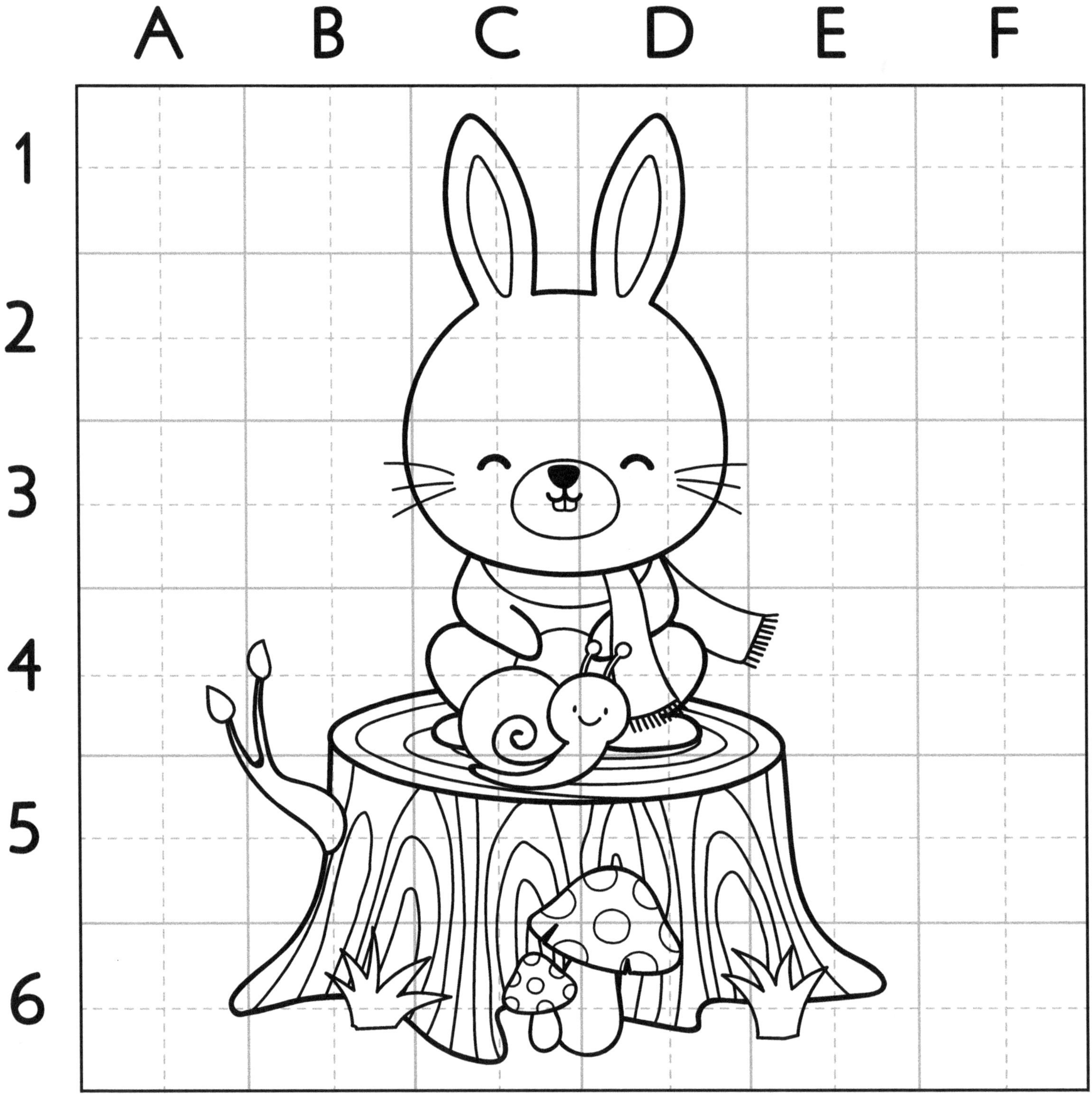

A B C D E F

1 2 3 4 5 6

Draw the picture in the grid

	A	B	C	D	E	F
1						
2						
3						
4						
5						
6						

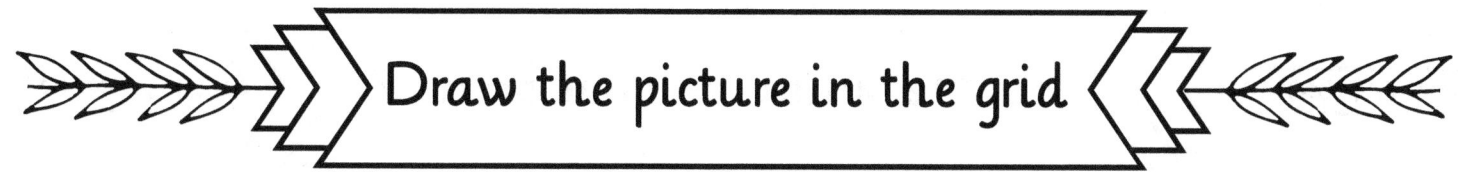

 Trace the bunny for more practice!

 Practice drawing the picture on your own!

Cat & Bunny

Draw the picture in the grid

	A	B	C	D	E	F
1						
2						
3						
4						
5						
6						

 Trace the cat & bunny for more practice!

 Practice drawing the picture on your own!

Corgis

A B C D E F

1
2
3
4
5
6

A B C D E F

1
2
3
4
5
6

 Trace the corgis for more practice!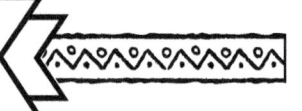

 Practice drawing the picture on your own!

Deer

Draw the picture in the grid

	A	B	C	D	E	F
1						
2						
3						
4						
5						
6						

 Trace the deer for more practice!

 Practice drawing the picture on your own!

Frog

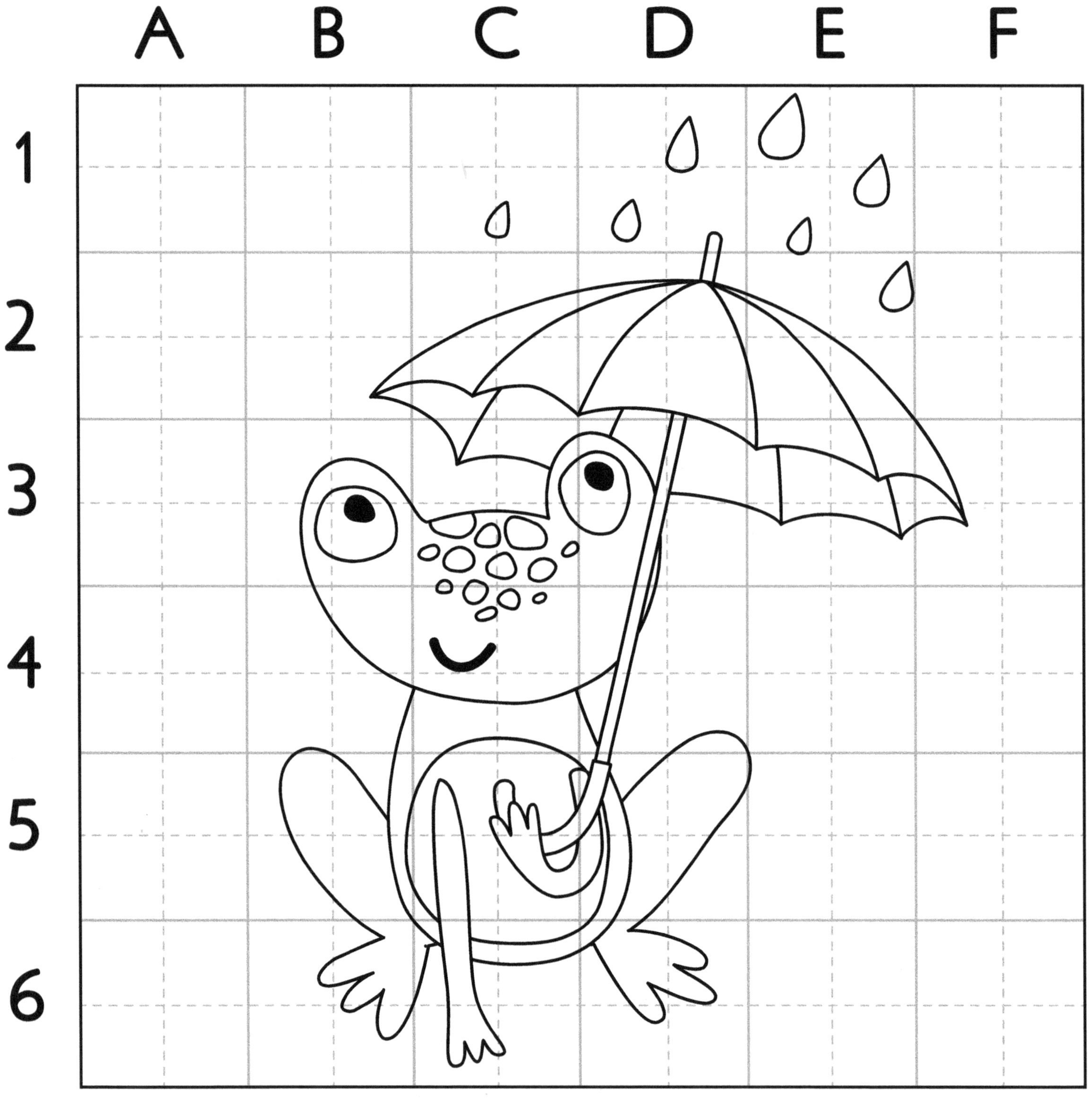

	A	B	C	D	E	F
1						
2						
3						
4						
5						
6						

Draw the picture in the grid

	A	B	C	D	E	F
1						
2						
3						
4						
5						
6						

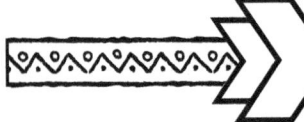 Trace the frog for more practice!

 Practice drawing the picture on your own!

Giraffe

    A   B   C   D   E   F

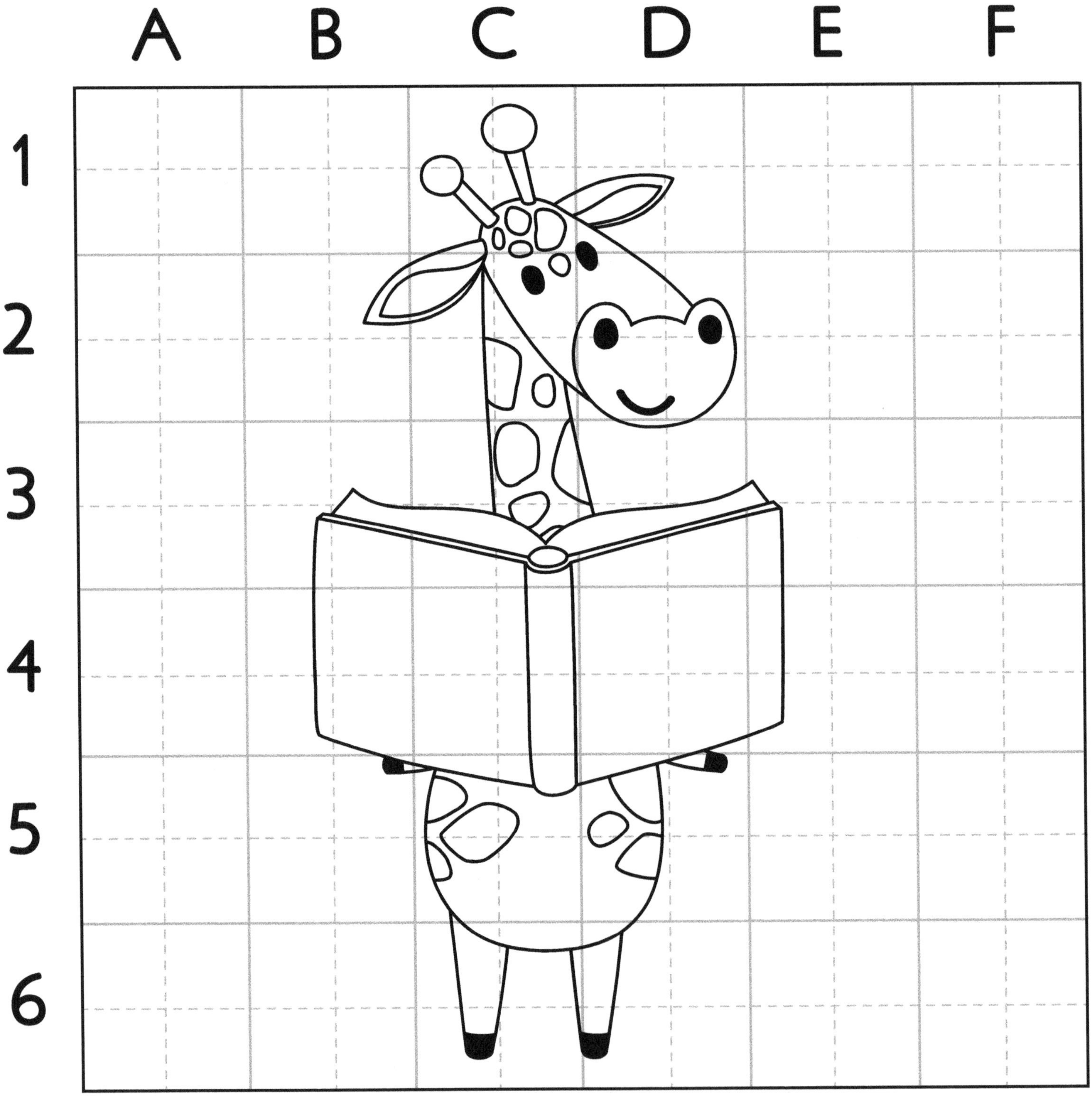

1
2
3
4
5
6

Draw the picture in the grid

A B C D E F

1
2
3
4
5
6

 Trace the giraffe for more practice!

 Practice drawing the picture on your own!

Horse & Princess

	A	B	C	D	E	F
1						
2						
3						
4						
5						
6						

Draw the picture in the grid

	A	B	C	D	E	F
1						
2						
3						
4						
5						
6						

 Trace the horse & the princess for more practice!

 Practice drawing the picture on your own!

Kangaroo

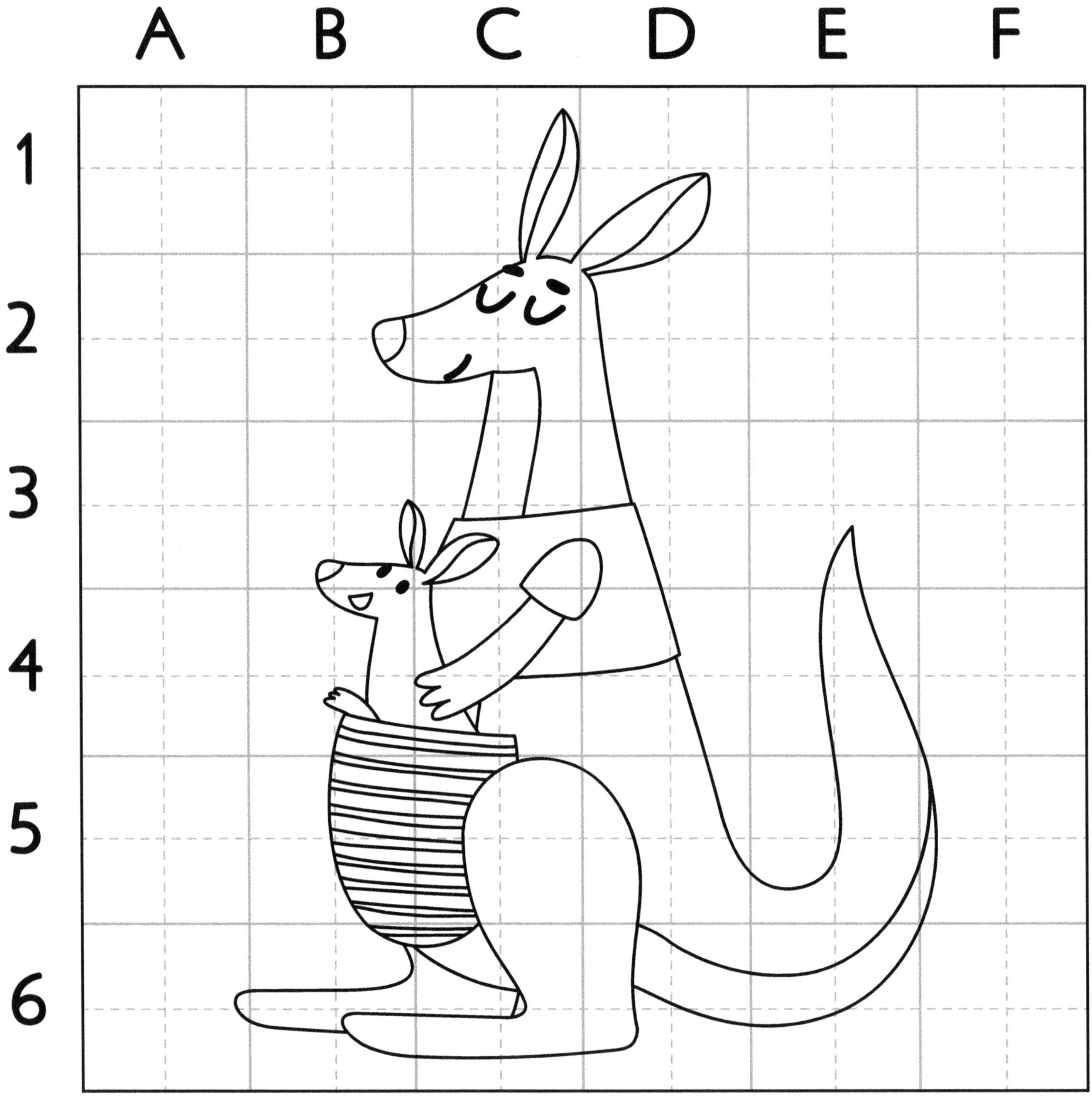

A B C D E F

1
2
3
4
5
6

 Practice drawing the picture on your own!

 Trace the kangaroo for more practice!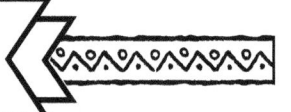

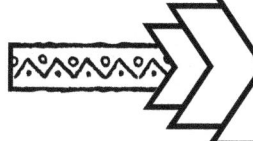 Practice drawing the picture on your own!

Koala

	A	B	C	D	E	F
1						
2						
3						
4						
5						
6						

Draw the picture in the grid

	A	B	C	D	E	F
1						
2						
3						
4						
5						
6						

 Trace the koala for more practice!

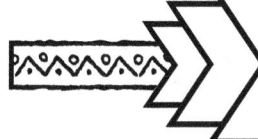 Practice drawing the picture on your own!

Llama

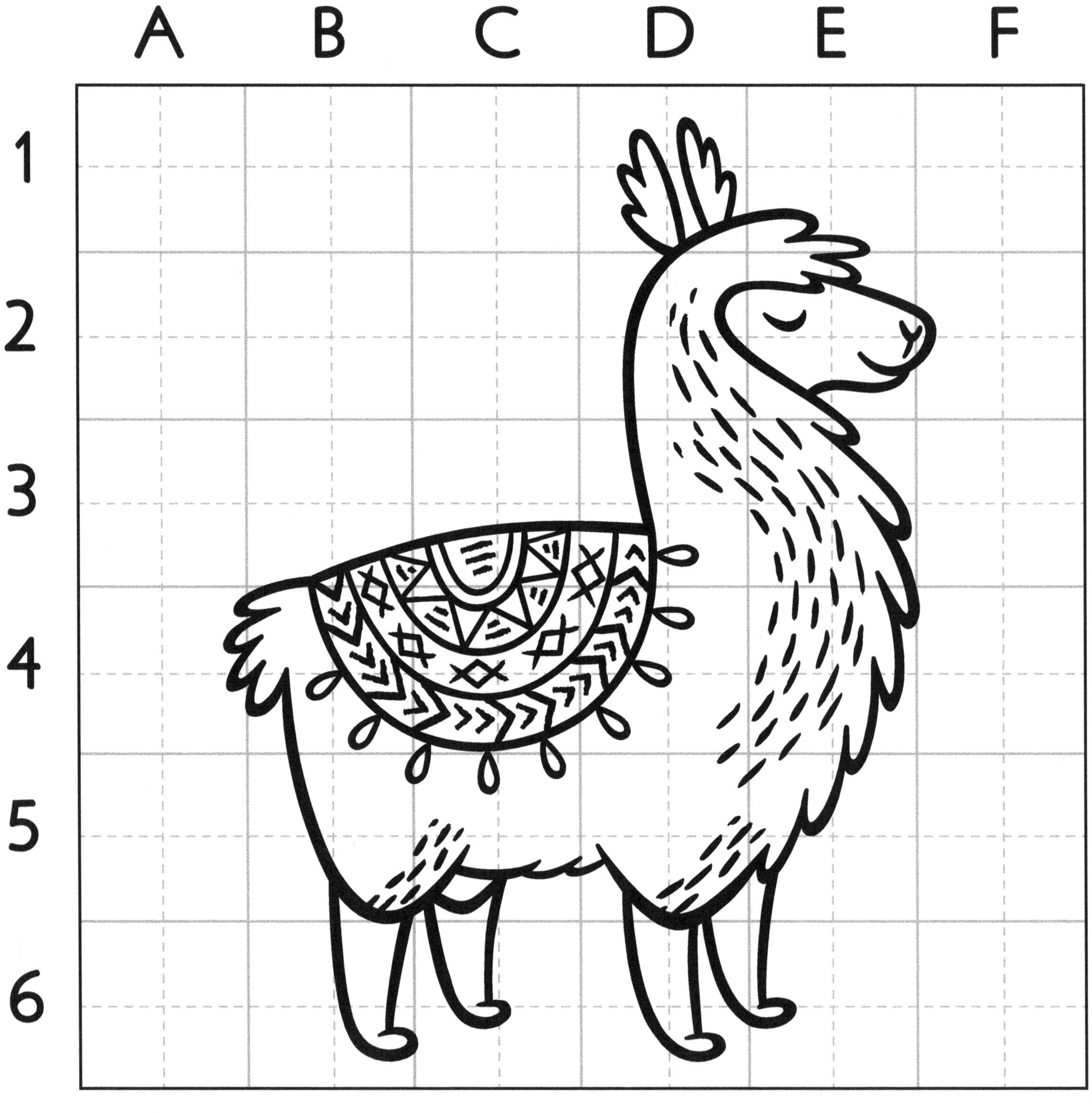

Draw the picture in the grid

	A	B	C	D	E	F
1						
2						
3						
4						
5						
6						

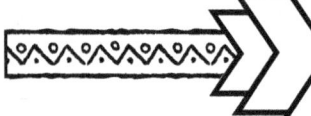 Trace the llama for more practice!

 Practice drawing the picture on your own!

Monkey

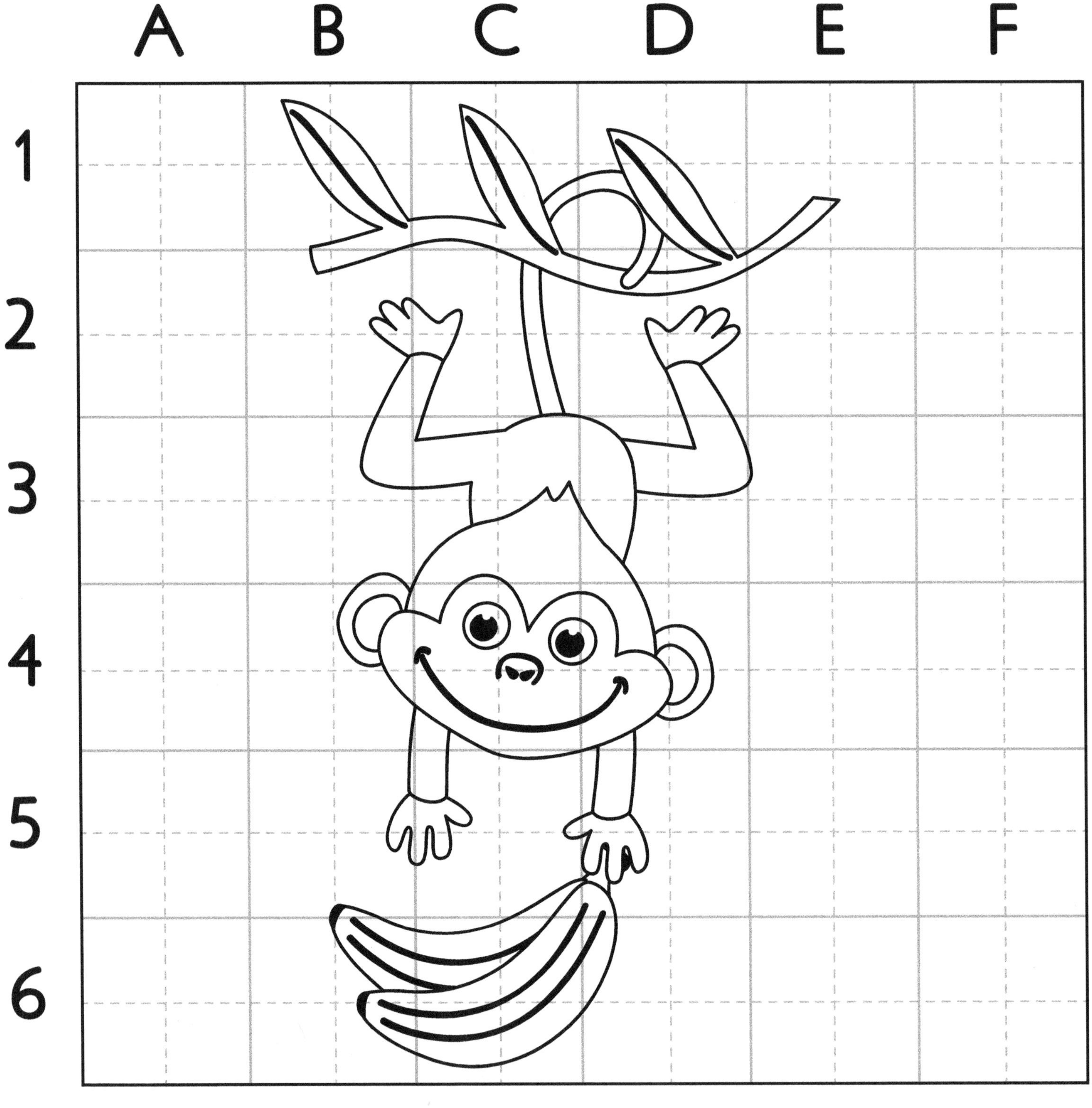

Draw the picture in the grid

	A	B	C	D	E	F
1						
2						
3						
4						
5						
6						

 Trace the monkey for more practice!

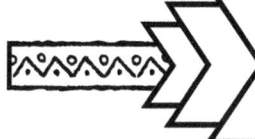 Practice drawing the picture on your own!

Owl

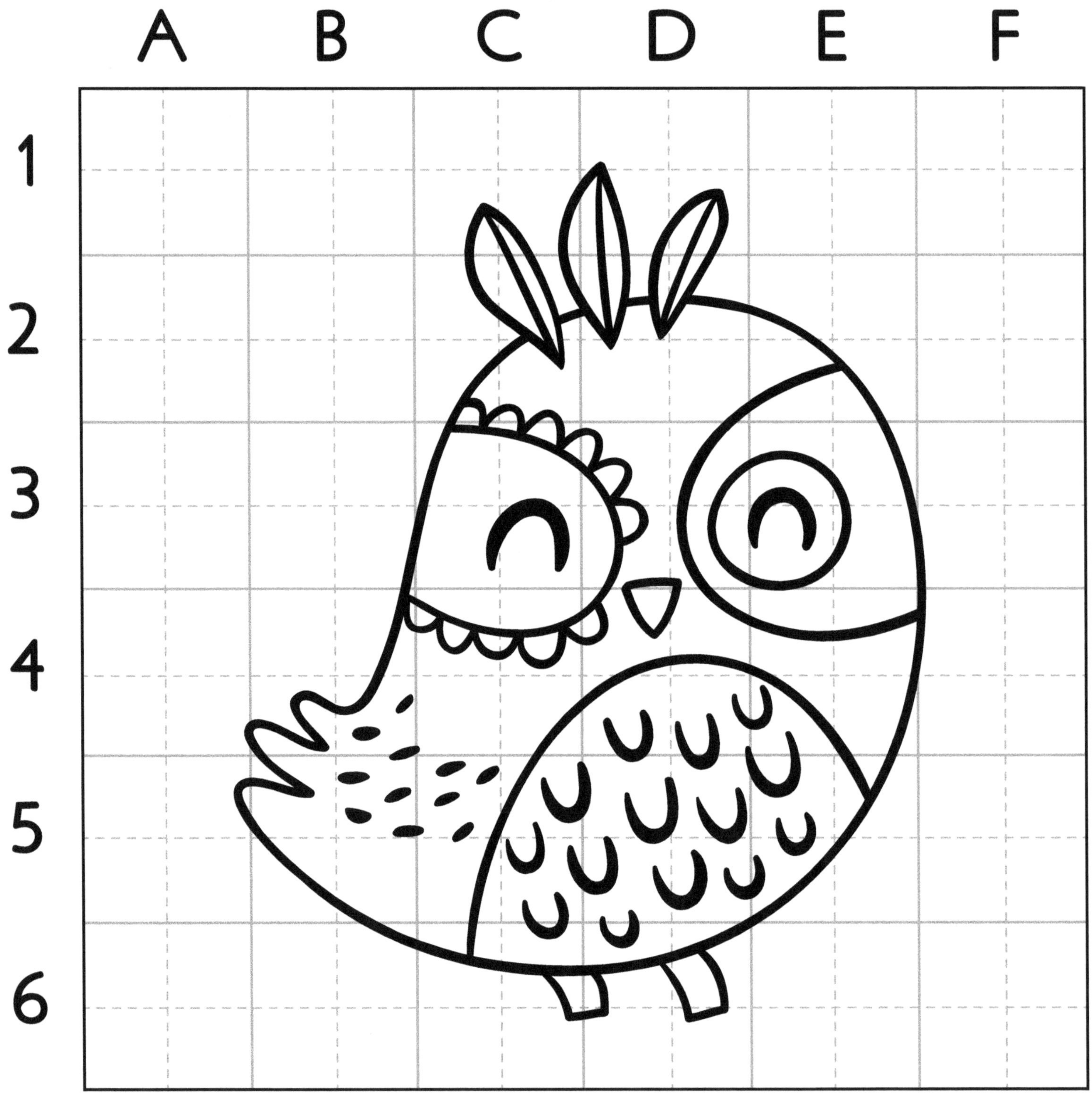

A B C D E F

1
2
3
4
5
6

Draw the picture in the grid

	A	B	C	D	E	F
1						
2						
3						
4						
5						
6						

 Trace the owl for more practice!

 Practice drawing the picture on your own!

Penguin

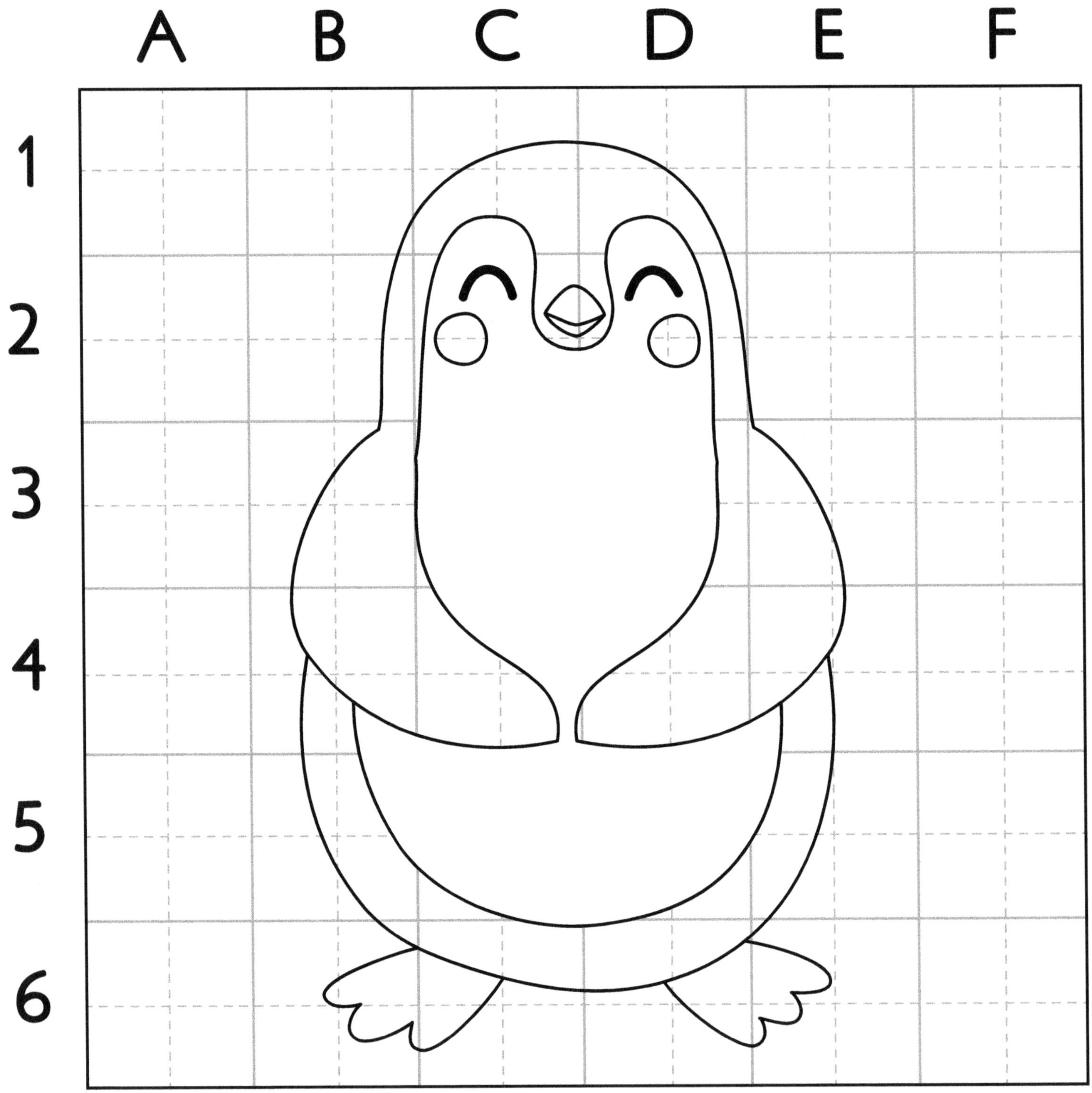

	A	B	C	D	E	F
1						
2						
3						
4						
5						
6						

Draw the picture in the grid

	A	B	C	D	E	F
1						
2						
3						
4						
5						
6						

 Trace the penguin for more practice!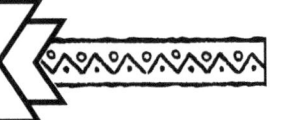

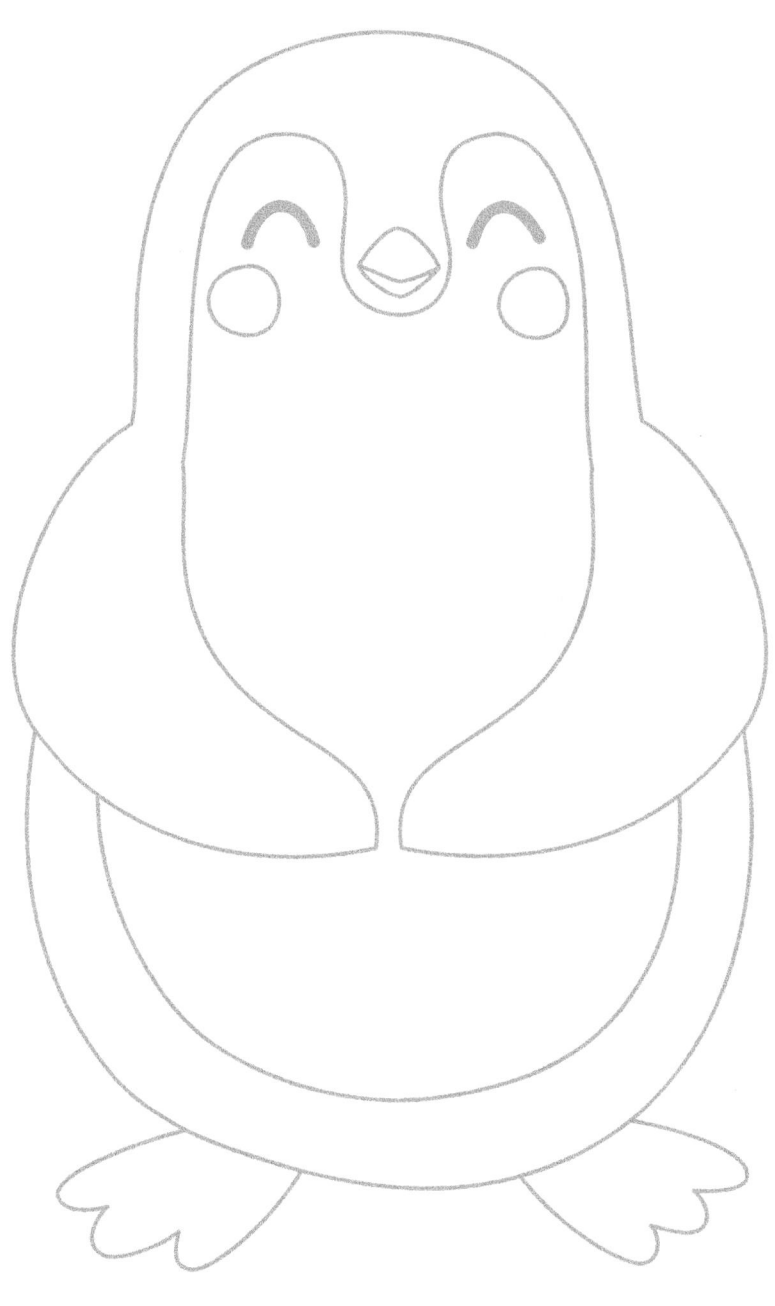

 Practice drawing the picture on your own!

Pig

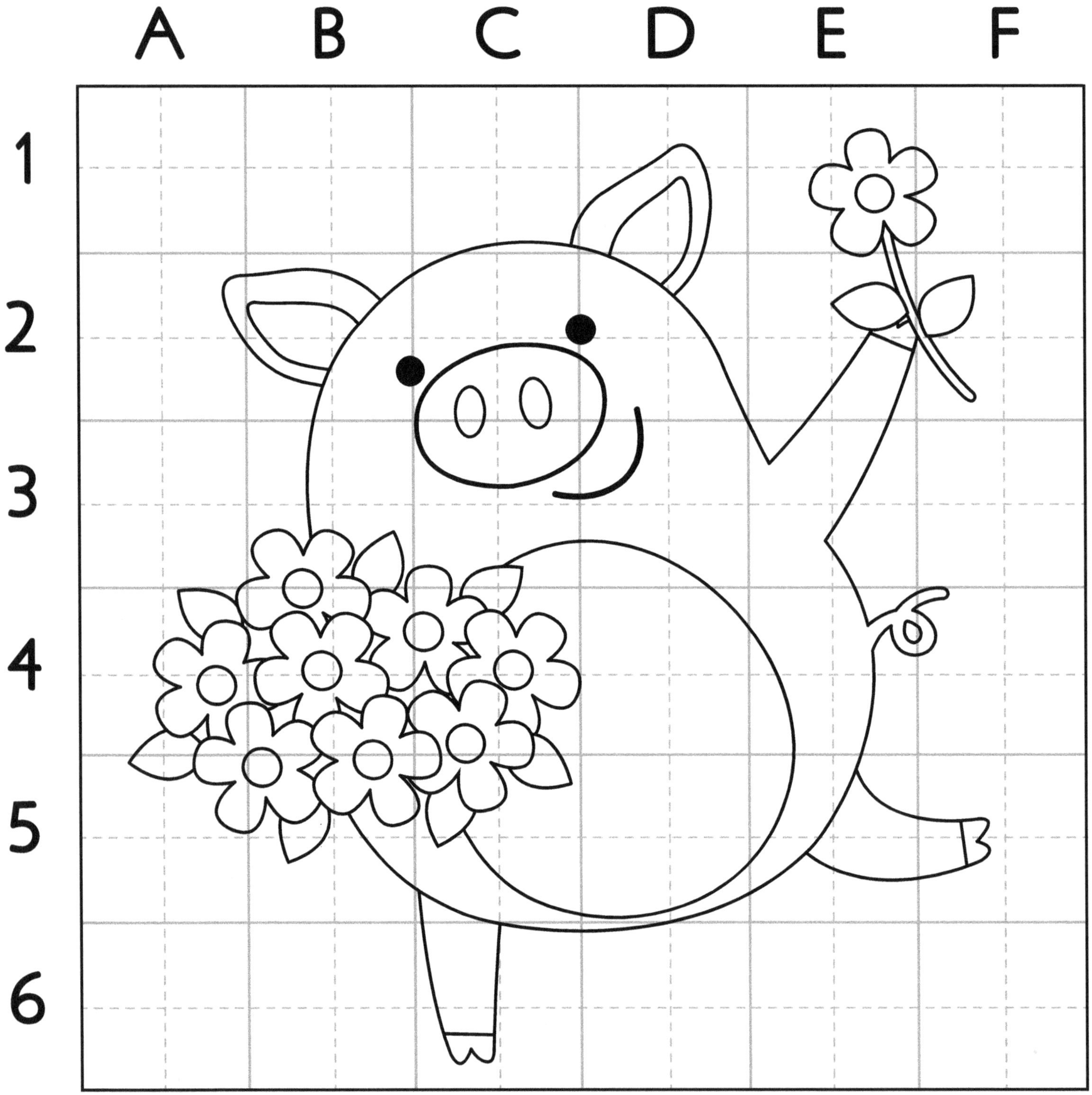

A B C D E F

1
2
3
4
5
6

Draw the picture in the grid

	A	B	C	D	E	F
1						
2						
3						
4						
5						
6						

Trace the pig for more practice!

 Practice drawing the picture on your own!

Polar Bears

	A	B	C	D	E	F
1						
2						
3						
4						
5						
6						

Draw the picture in the grid

	A	B	C	D	E	F
1						
2						
3						
4						
5						
6						

 Trace the polar bears for more practice!

 Practice drawing the picture on your own!

Rhino

	A	B	C	D	E	F
1						
2						
3						
4						
5						
6						

Draw the picture in the grid

	A	B	C	D	E	F
1						
2						
3						
4						
5						
6						

 Trace the rhino for more practice!

 Practice drawing the picture on your own!

Seals

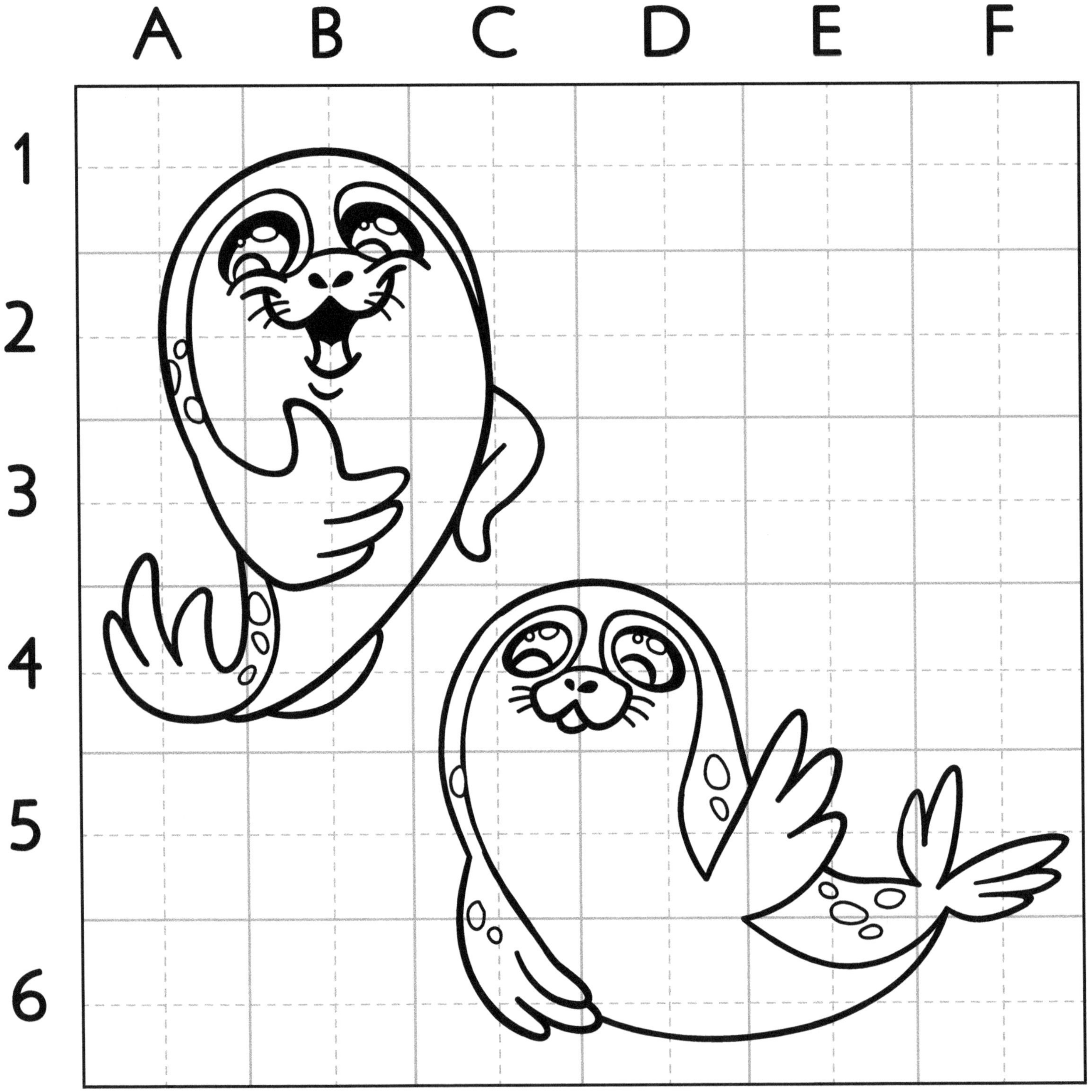

	A	B	C	D	E	F
1						
2						
3						
4						
5						
6						

Draw the picture in the grid

	A	B	C	D	E	F
1						
2						
3						
4						
5						
6						

 Trace the seals for more practice!

 Practice drawing the picture on your own!

Sloth

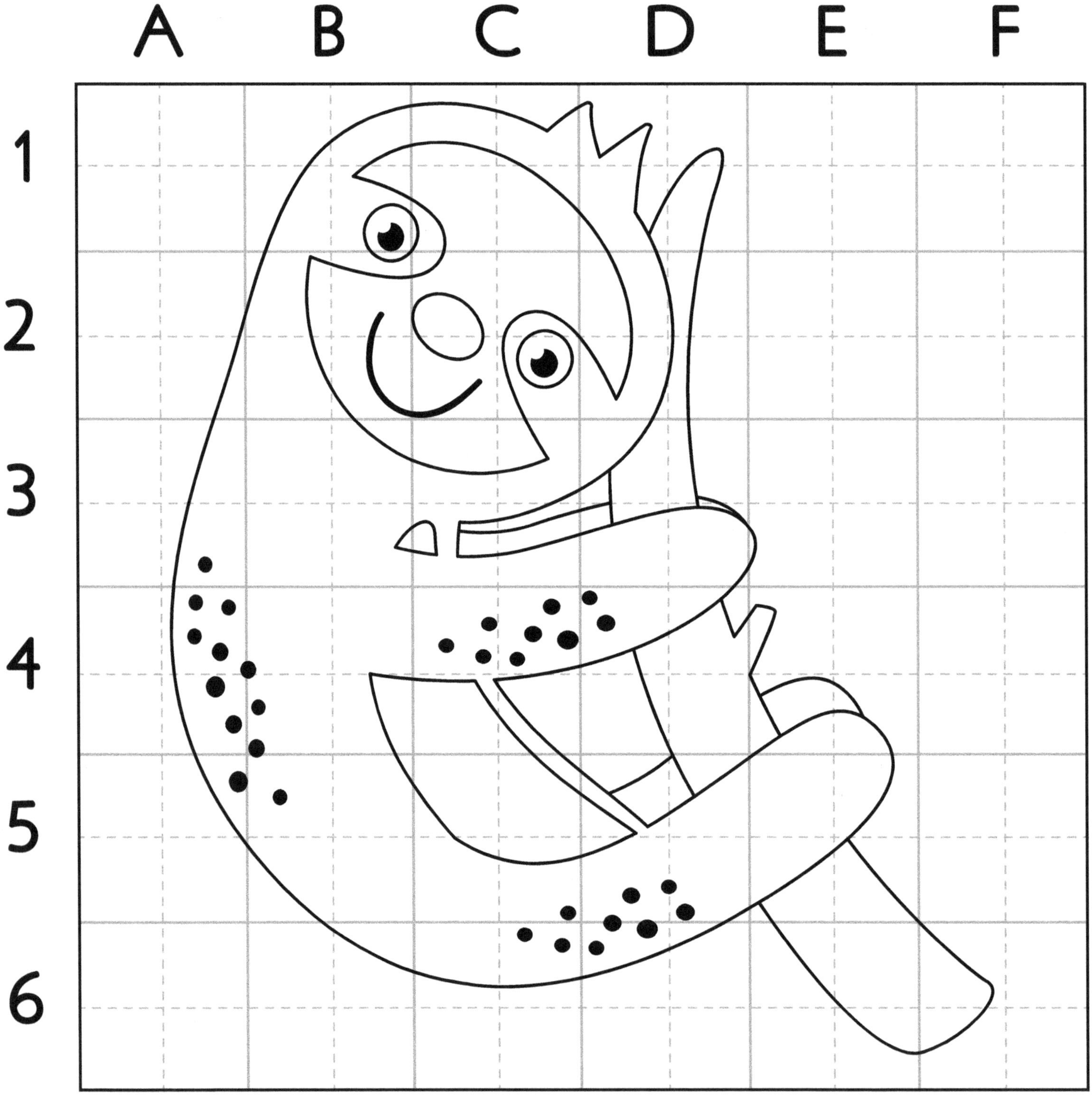

Draw the picture in the grid

	A	B	C	D	E	F
1						
2						
3						
4						
5						
6						

Trace the sloath for more practice!

 Practice drawing the picture on your own!

Snail

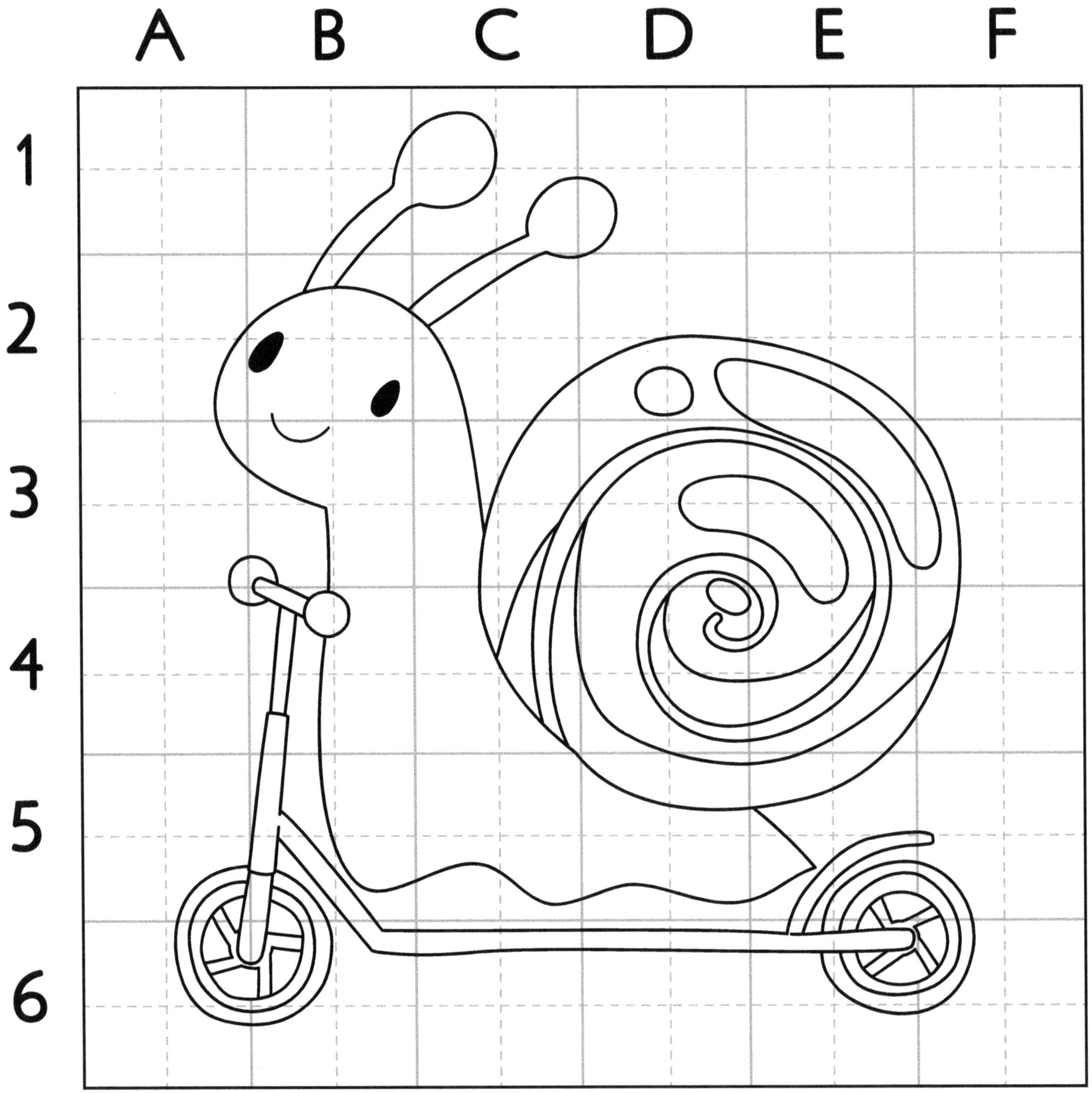

```
    A    B    C    D    E    F
1
2
3
4
5
6
```

Draw the picture in the grid

	A	B	C	D	E	F
1						
2						
3						
4						
5						
6						

 Trace the snail for more practice!

 Practice drawing the picture on your own!

Squirrel

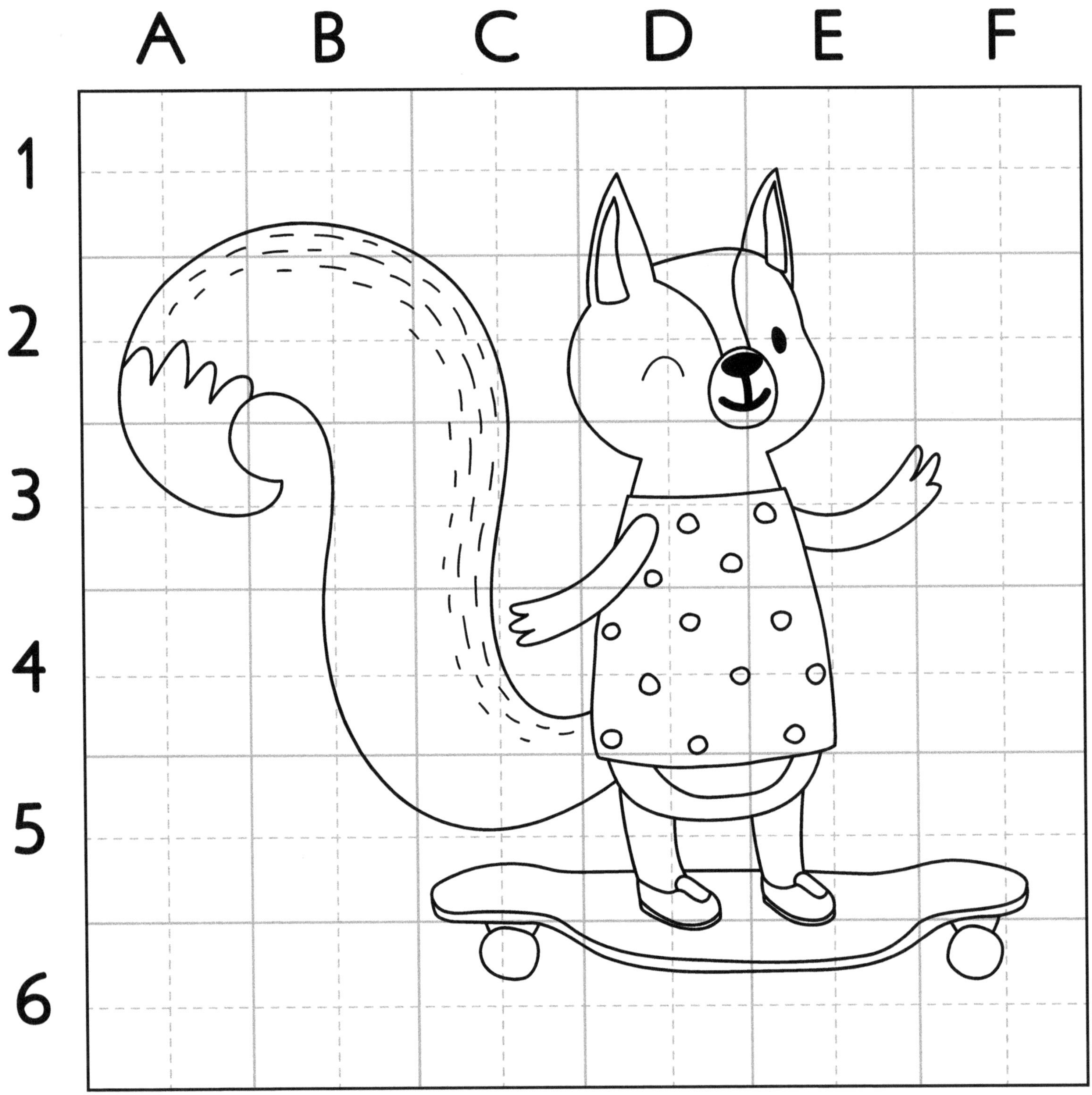

Draw the picture in the grid

	A	B	C	D	E	F
1						
2						
3						
4						
5						
6						

 Trace the squirrel for more practice!

 Practice drawing the picture on your own!

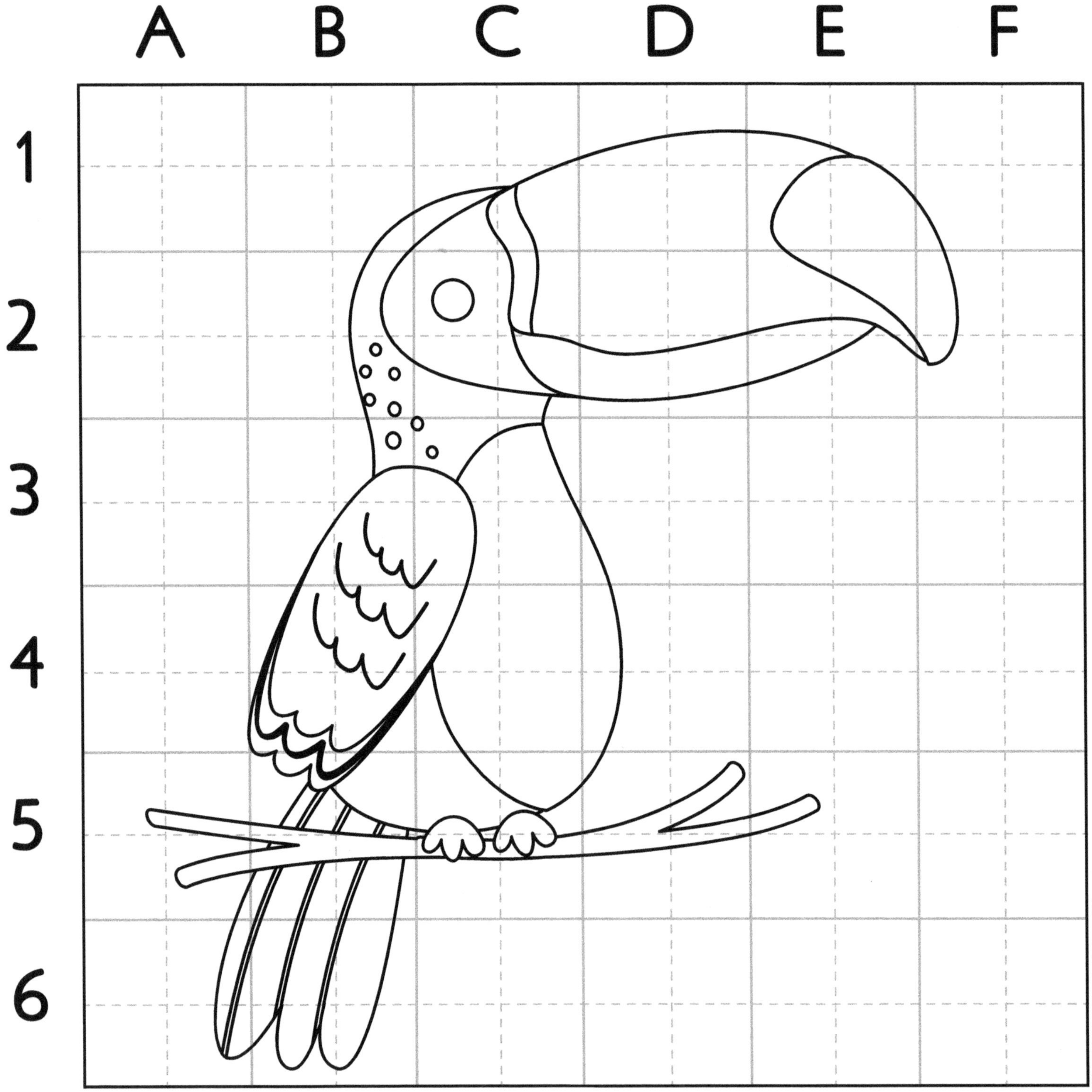

Draw the picture in the grid

	A	B	C	D	E	F
1						
2						
3						
4						
5						
6						

 Trace the toucan for more practice!

 Practice drawing the picture on your own!

# Turtles

Draw the picture in the grid

	A	B	C	D	E	F
1						
2						
3						
4						
5						
6						

Trace the turtles for more practice!

 Practice drawing the picture on your own!

Cat

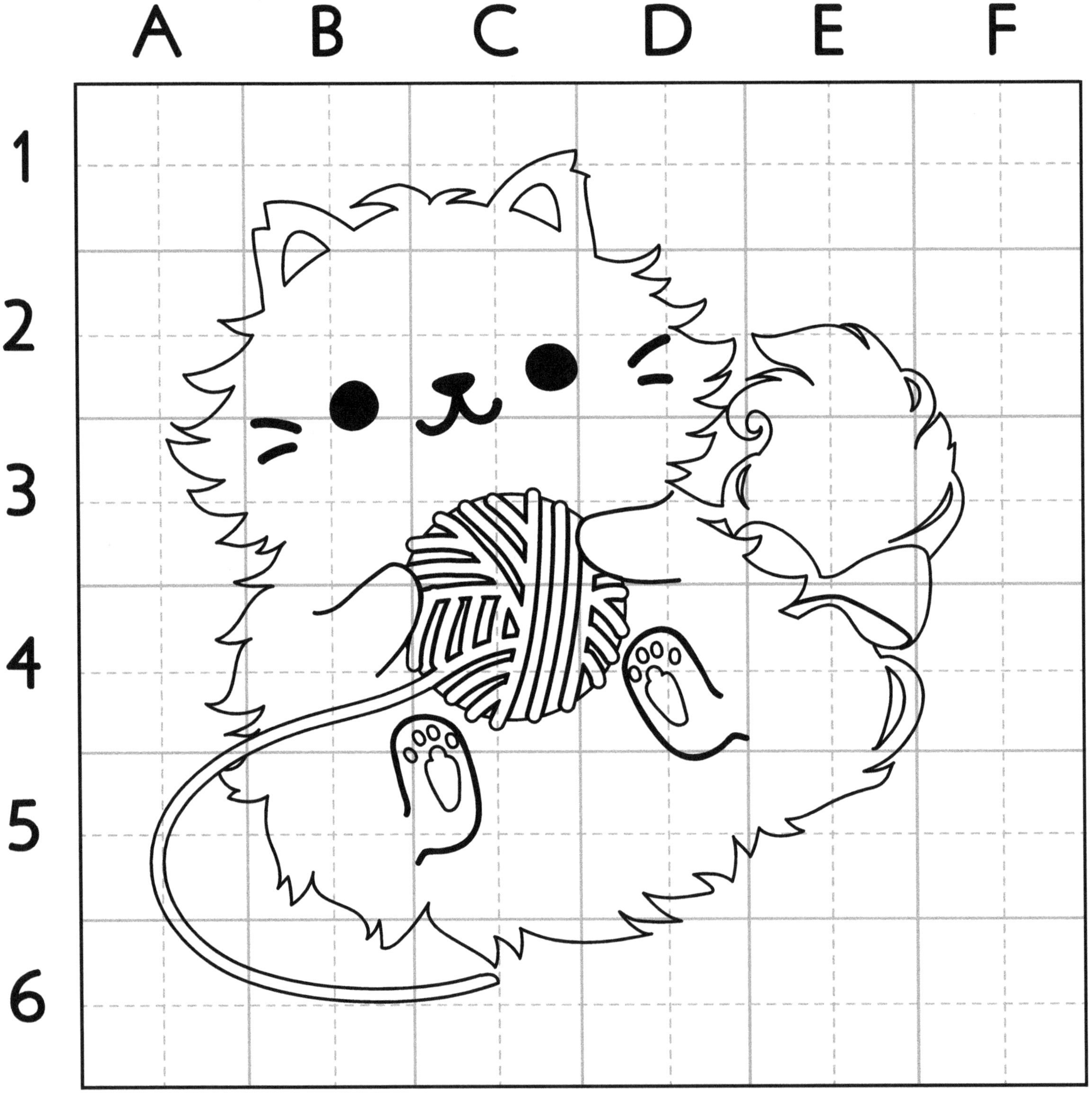

A B C D E F

1
2
3
4
5
6

Draw the picture in the grid

	A	B	C	D	E	F
1						
2						
3						
4						
5						
6						

 Trace the cat for more practice!

 Practice drawing the picture on your own!

Elephant

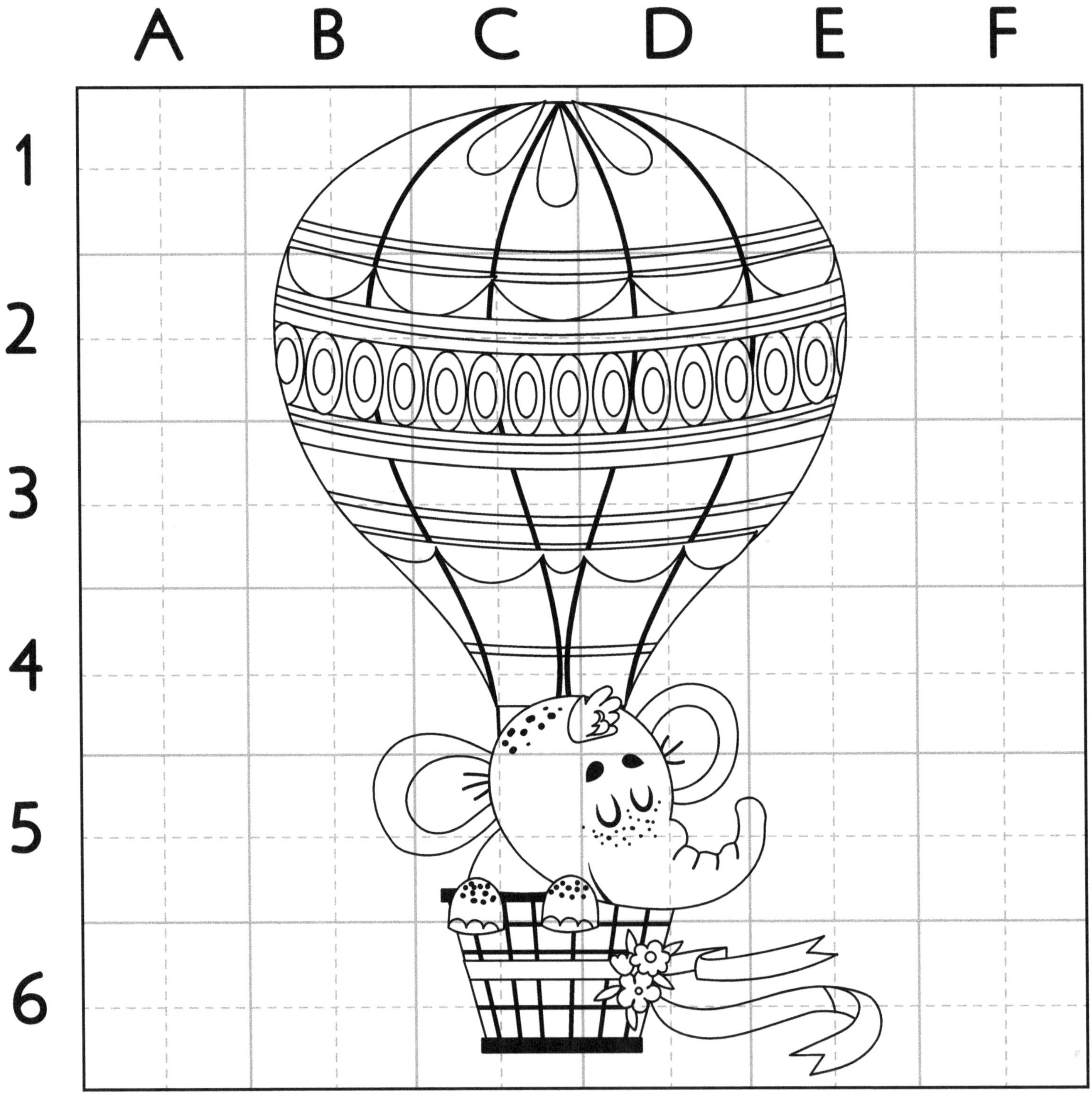

Draw the picture in the grid

	A	B	C	D	E	F
1						
2						
3						
4						
5						
6						

 Trace the elephant for more practice!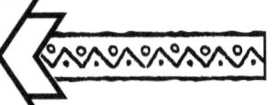

 Practice drawing the picture on your own!

Mouse

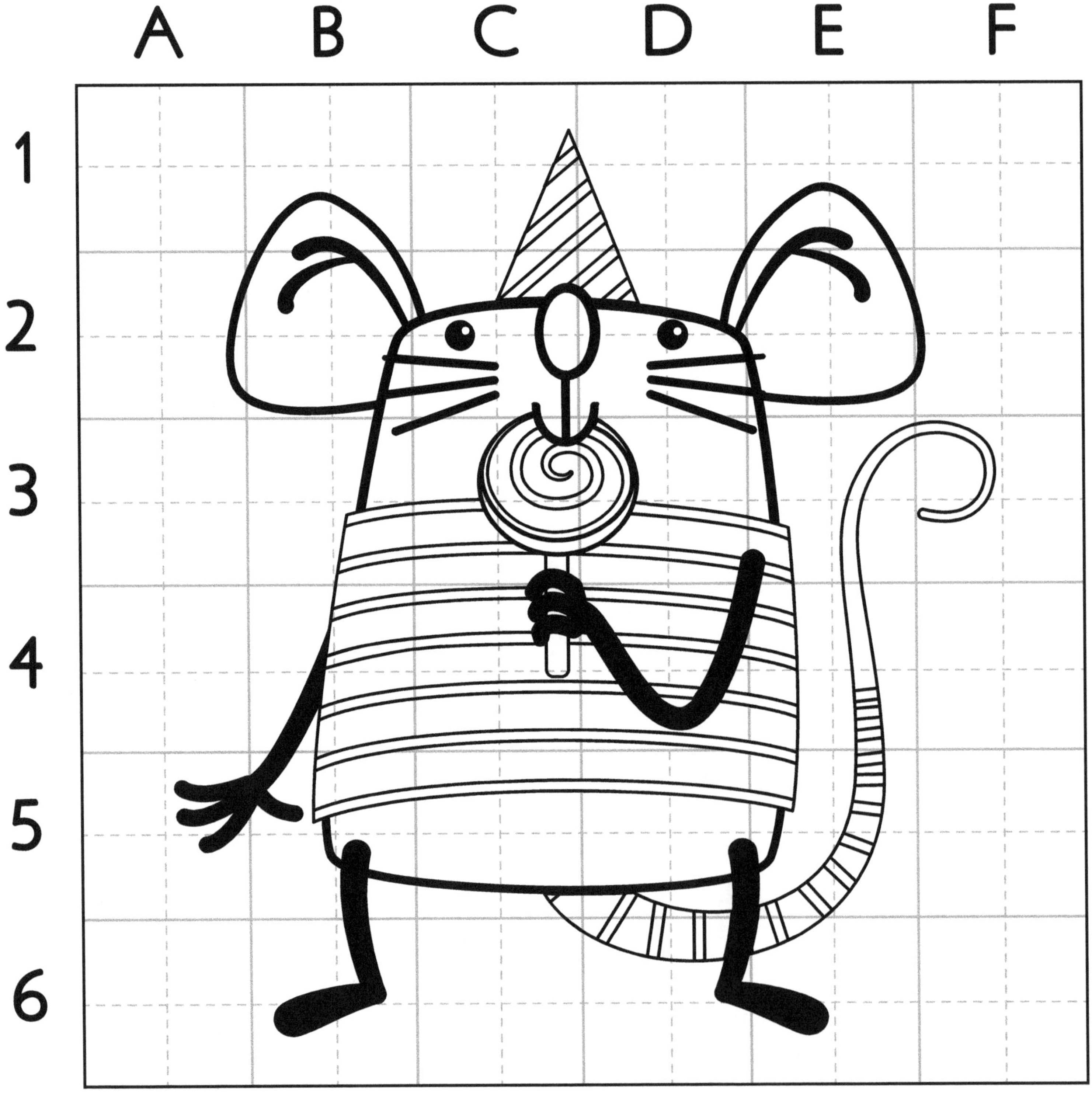

	A	B	C	D	E	F
1						
2						
3						
4						
5						
6						

Draw the picture in the grid

	A	B	C	D	E	F
1						
2						
3						
4						
5						
6						

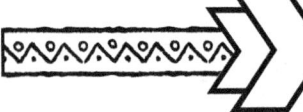 Trace the mouse for more practice!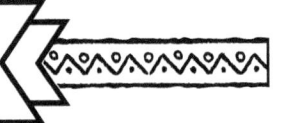

 Practice drawing the picture on your own!

A Special Request

Thank you wholeheartedly for purchasing *How to Draw Animals*. Now that you've got the book, we have a small favor to ask of you and it will only take a moment of your time. After your child has had a chance to dive in, get drawing, and really had an opportunity to enjoy the book, we ask that you please share a review of your purchase with other potential buyers.

The success of both this book and H.R. Wallace Publishing really depends upon generous people like you who take the take the time to share their reviews. After all, it's only by garnering a considerable number of reviews that this title can really hope to compete with bigger publishing houses that have a much larger marketing budget than we do.

So, please visit the product page for this book and then leave a review. We will be ever so grateful, because your support really is paramount to our success.

Above all else, we hope you and your child are happy with the book and that it provides hours of drawing fun.

www.ingramcontent.com/pod-product-compliance
Lightning Source LLC
Chambersburg PA
CBHW080940040426
42444CB00015B/3386